Dear Nathaniel

Hope you will enjoy reading this story.

Love to you always,

Grampa & Grama White

THE REAL STORY OF THE EXODUS

THE REAL STORY OF
THE EXODUS

by PAUL L. MAIER

Illustrated by Gerad Taylor

CONCORDIA PUBLISHING HOUSE • SAINT LOUIS

Published by Concordia Publishing House
3558 S. Jefferson Avenue • St. Louis, MO 63118-3968
1-800-325-3040 • www.cph.org

Text © 2009 by Paul L. Maier
Illustrations © 2009 Concordia Publishing House

1 2 3 4 5 6 7 8 9 10   18 17 16 15 14 13 12 11 10 09

Long after the great flood, many different people were again living on the earth. God remembered His promise given to our first parents, Adam and Eve, to send a Savior, and so God chose one group of people to fulfill this promise. He selected the descendents of Noah's son Shem, who would later be called the Hebrews.

Near the Persian Gulf in southern Mesopotamia, there was a city called Ur. A man named Abraham lived there. In a dream, God told Abraham to leave the many false gods and goddesses in Ur and travel westward to the land of Canaan. This was at the edge of the Mediterranean Sea, and there, the Lord promised, he would be the founder of that great nation of people He had chosen.

And so it happened. Abraham and his wife, Sarah, made the trip to this Promised Land and had a baby named Isaac. Later on, Isaac had a son named Jacob, who had no less than twelve sons of his own. But Canaan was hit with a terrible famine, so those twelve sons and their families moved to Egypt to stay alive. There they prospered and started growing into the great nation God had promised.

CHAPTER ONE

Then Pharaoh commanded all of his people, "Every son that is born to the Hebrews you shall cast into the Nile, but you shall let every daughter live." Exodus 1:22

At first, the kings of Egypt—they were called pharaohs—were kind to their Hebrew guests and let them live in a richly fertile section of the Nile Delta called Goshen. But after several centuries, the mood changed. A new dynasty of Egyptian pharaohs feared the growing numbers of the Hebrews. What if they should join Egypt's enemies and try to take over the country?

The pharaoh came up with a very brutal solution: he threw the Hebrews into slavery and ordered that every baby boy of theirs should be slaughtered! That would cut down the race and end the danger—so he thought.

But the Lord had other plans and would now save His chosen people. A very special baby boy was born to one of the Hebrew families in Egypt. So he wouldn't be killed, his mother took something like a big picnic basket, waterproofed its bottom and sides, and turned it into a tiny model of Noah's ark. Commending her baby to God, she put him inside this mini boat and floated it into some reeds along the banks of the Nile.

A daughter of the pharaoh and her attendants, who were bathing at the shore downstream, noticed the little craft stuck in the reeds and retrieved it. They were shocked to find a crying baby inside. Not only did the princess save it, she adopted the infant and called him Moses, which means "drawn from the water" in the Hebrew language and "son" in Egyptian.

CHAPTER TWO

When Pharaoh heard of it, he sought to kill Moses. But Moses fled from Pharaoh and stayed in the land of Midian. Exodus 2:15

Wait—it gets better. The daughter of the pharaoh needed someone to nurse little Moses. Moses' older sister, Miriam, came on the scene and suggested that "one of the Hebrew women" might do this. And so it happened that baby Moses came back to his own mother! Chance? Coincidence? Or was God involved?

Moses was raised as a member of the royal family of Egypt. But princes get into trouble, and Moses was no exception. One day, he saw an Egyptian beating up a Hebrew worker. Moses was furious, lost control of himself, and killed the Egyptian. To avoid arrest, he fled eastward into the Sinai desert, where he lived as a shepherd, tending the flocks of a man named Jethro. In fact, Jethro soon become his father-in-law, since Moses married his daughter Zipporah.

Meanwhile, God had not forgotten the slavery of His people. One day, Moses saw something on the side of Mount Sinai that made no sense: a bush was on fire, yet it never burned up! Flames just kept shooting out of it. Suddenly, the voice of God announced from the flames how the Hebrews would be rescued from Egypt: "You, Moses, will go to Pharaoh and tell him, 'Let My people go!'"

"Me, Lord?" Moses stammered. "I'm supposed to do this?"

God easily took care of Moses' objection that he had no speaking talent. He simply told him to take along his older brother, Aaron, as spokesman. Aaron had a way with words.

CHAPTER THREE

Still, Pharaoh's heart was hardened, and he would not listen to them, as the Lord had said. Exodus 7:13

What a dramatic scene! The pharaoh of the sprawling Egyptian Empire, which extended from the Sahara Desert to Mesopotamia, sat on his throne, glaring at two Hebrew visitors from the desert. What could they possibly want from the master of the world?

"God has instructed us to tell you, Pharaoh," said Moses, "'Let My people go so they may serve Me in the wilderness!'"

"I'm supposed to believe that?" The pharaoh laughed.

Moses now provided the miraculous sign that the Lord had given him back at the burning bush. "By this you shall know that we were sent by God," said Moses. Aaron threw down his shepherd's rod, and it turned into a slithering snake! Gasps of surprise erupted from the king's court.

But the pharaoh clapped his hands and brought in some court magicians, who tried to imitate what Aaron had done. They also seemed to have rods and snakes, and the king smiled, as if to say, "We can do that trick too." When Aaron's rod attacked and ate up the other rods, however, the pharaoh quit smiling.

Again, and in the name of God, Moses demanded that the Hebrews be set free from their slavery. Again the pharaoh refused.

God would find other ways.

CHAPTER FOUR

Then the Lord said to Moses, "Go in to Pharaoh and say to him, 'Thus says the Lord, "Let My people go, that they may serve Me." ' " Exodus 8:1

A series of horrible plagues now swept across Egypt. Nature became unbalanced, and its creatures grew in monstrous numbers to attack man and beast. Aaron waved his rod over the Nile River, and the water turned into blood, fouling the waters and killing the fish. Some people have suggested that God caused a bloom of toxic red algae or had red sediment wash down from cliffs further up the Nile. People madly dug wells for drinkable water to quench their thirst. But the pharaoh ignored God's sign.

A week later, vast swarms of frogs crawled out of the Nile and its canals, jumping into the homes and beds of Egypt and even into the palace itself. This rattled the pharaoh, and he promised Moses he would let the people leave if the frogs did. The frogs all died (and never was there such a smell of decay in Egypt). But then the pharaoh went back on his word and kept the people in slavery, so more plagues were necessary.

Next, the very dust of Egypt turned into gnats that crawled over everyone, and after that swarms of flies darkened all the land of Egypt except Goshen, where the Hebrews lived. The fifth plague then killed all the Egyptians' livestock. And the sixth afflicted humans as well, whose skin now broke out in painful boils.

Hail and furious thunderstorms were the seventh plague, clouds of locusts the eighth, and a dreadful darkness the ninth—in a land that worshiped the sun. The pharaoh observed that none of these affected Goshen, where the Hebrews lived, but after each plague, he still stubbornly refused to release the Hebrews.

CHAPTER FIVE

It is the sacrifice of the Lord's Passover, for He passed over the houses of the people of Israel in Egypt, when He struck the Egyptians but spared our houses. Exodus 12:27

Finally, God had enough of these broken promises. Moses warned the pharaoh that the worst plague of all was coming. In every household across the land of Egypt, the firstborn son—the heir apparent and the family's hope for the future—would die. The pharaoh refused to believe it—until it happened.

Moses now assembled all the Israelites (another name for the Hebrew people at that time). He announced that the day of liberation had come at last and that they would escape from Egypt with the Almighty's help. They were to pack all their belongings and eat a special dinner that night that included roast lamb, unleavened bread, and bitter herbs. The blood of the lamb was to be painted over the doorposts and lintels of their homes, so that when the angel of death took the firstborns, it would pass over all doorways painted in this way. This is why that special supper was called the Passover, and it is celebrated to this very day.

So began the most terrible night in history. Ghastly moaning arose in all homes across the land, except those of the Hebrews. Crying was loudest at the royal palace, since the eldest son of the pharaoh himself was stricken and died. In desperation, the king summoned Moses and told him to take his people and leave Egypt immediately. This time, the pharaoh did not change his mind.

An immense crowd of Israelites, singing praises of thanksgiving to God, now started on their great Exodus—the journey from Egypt to the Promised Land.

CHAPTER SIX

And Miriam sang to them: "Sing to the LORD, for He has triumphed gloriously; the horse and his rider He has thrown into the sea."
Exodus 15:21

The joyful Hebrews traveled eastward across the Nile Delta toward the Red Sea and the Sinai desert. They would have to cross both to reach the homeland of their ancestors. But just as they reached the shores of the Red Sea (actually, the "Reed Sea" in Hebrew) came awful news. Once again, the pharaoh had gone back on his word. He was now leading the Egyptian army against them to prevent their escape. Fleeing further eastward was impossible, since they were standing at the edge of the sea. Terrified, the Hebrews were caught in a terrible trap.

But then Moses announced to his people, "Fear not, stand firm, and see the salvation of the LORD!" (Exodus 14:13). He stretched out his hand and held it over the sea. A powerful east wind roared over the waters, parting them on both sides to create a roadway across the sea bottom! Overjoyed, the Hebrews walked across that roadway all the way to the other side.

When the pharaoh and his army saw what a convenient highway that was, they tried it also. Once they were halfway across, however, the walls of water on both sides came crashing down on them, drowning all of the Egyptians.

But the Israelites were safely on the other side. The Lord had performed another spectacular miracle to save His people! Moses and the people joined in a song of thanksgiving, while his sister, Miriam, led the women in singing and dancing. It was the greatest moment in Hebrew history.

CHAPTER SEVEN

And the LORD said to Moses, "I have heard the grumbling of the people of Israel."
Exodus 16:11–12

Crossing the Sinai desert was no easy trip. Even in spring, it is very hot there. And can you imagine the task of trying to keep 600,000 fed (and that was only the men)? When people are hungry and thirsty, they get angry. Although they were now free people and safe from their enemies, the Hebrews started complaining. One yelled out, "Has God saved us from the Egyptians only to let us die out here in the wilderness?" "I wish we'd never left Egypt!" cried another.

Moses heard the murmurings and asked the Lord for help. During their long trek across the desert, God was very close to His people, as symbolized by a lofty pillar of fire that protected them at night and a column of cloud by day. When they reached an oasis at a place called Marah and tried to drink the water, they spat it out because it was bitter. God told Moses to throw a tree into the water, and it became drinkable. Other oases, like the one at Elim, had good wells and water.

That took care of their thirst, but what about food? Each morning, God had a tasty white substance called manna descend to the ground in quantities enough to feed them all. The Israelites were surprised at food like this and asked, "Manna?" which means "What is this?" in Hebrew. The name stuck.

But what about protein? Every evening, great waves of quail flew over the camps of the Hebrews and landed, enough for their daily needs. God the Creator was also God the Preserver.

CHAPTER EIGHT

*The L*ORD *said to Moses, "Come up to Me on the mountain and wait*
there, and I will give you the tables of stone, with the law and the
commandment." Exodus 24:12

After several months of this grueling journey, the Israelites camped on
a broad plain in front of a lofty mountain called Sinai. God informed Moses that
this was where He would reveal the great rules that should guide the daily life of
His people. Because the mountain was sacred, no one was to approach and touch
it—except for Moses, who was to climb to its summit and receive God's rules.

While the Hebrews waited below, Moses climbed ever higher. He had
incredible courage, because Mount Sinai itself responded to the extraordinary
presence of God with lightning, thunder, fire, and smoke. For forty days,
Moses conversed with the Almighty, who gave him two sacred tablets of stone on
which were engraved His divine rules.

Later, these rules would be called the Ten Commandments. God's people
were to worship Him alone, the only God there is, and never bow down to idols
or use His name needlessly. They were to set aside one day each week—
the Sabbath—in which to give Him special worship. They were to honor their
parents and elders, never kill or be impure with anyone, and never steal or tell
lies about people or even be jealous of them.

Only the genius of God Himself could have created such a list of dos and
don'ts. Those ten commands would be at the heart of almost every law code that
would ever be devised, anywhere in the world.

And the Lᴏʀᴅ said to Moses, "Go down, for your people, whom you brought up out of the land of Egypt, have corrupted themselves." Exodus 32:7

Moses now climbed back down Mount Sinai, carrying the two stone panels with the divine laws engraved on them. But he was in for a terrible shock.

The people had grown impatient waiting for Moses to return. Some of the same hotheads who had complained earlier went to Moses' brother, Aaron, and demanded that he make gods for them because, as they put it, "We don't know what's happened to Moses." Many other voices supported that outrageous request.

Aaron, of course, should have rejected it with righteous fury. But he must have taken leave of his wits, because he actually had the people hand over their rings and golden jewelry, which he melted down and fashioned into the shape of a golden calf. Pagan Egyptians used animal forms to represent their gods, and now the Hebrews, too, worshiped this ridiculous idol with singing and dancing.

Moses saw it all and was enraged. He threw down the two tablets of God's Law, which broke into pieces much as the Israelites had also just broken the divine laws. Then he ground the calf into powder, scattered it onto water, and made the rebellious people drink it.

Returning up Mount Sinai, Moses asked the Lord to forgive His wayward people. In His gracious mercy, God did so and gave Moses a second copy of the Law to replace the one in pieces.

CHAPTER TEN

All the craftsmen among the workmen made the tabernacle with ten curtains. Exodus 36:8

The Lord gave many other instructions to Moses besides the Ten Commandments. With His people so prone to sin and error, they needed a clear road map for their lives and especially for how they were to worship Him.

Later in history, God would be served in a magnificent temple in Jerusalem, constructed by King Solomon. But now the Israelites were still traveling in the wilderness, so something of a portable temple was necessary. Under divine direction, the tabernacle filled that role: a large, richly adorned tent they constructed and could move from place to place on their journey. Taking acacia wood and covering it with gold, they crafted the ark of the covenant and placed it inside the tabernacle. It contained the two stone tablets of divine Law, the Ten Commandments.

God also gave Moses exact specifications for arranging an altar for incense, lampstands, tables, priestly garments, veils, and curtains. He provided a calendar for the three sacred festivals to be celebrated each year and a schedule for offerings and sacrifices. Civil, criminal, social, and even medical ordinances were also part of God's directions for governing the lives of the Israelites.

Aaron, of course, should have been punished for his terrible behavior with the golden calf, but the Lord not only forgave him, He established a priesthood for Aaron and his descendants.

We surely have a merciful God!

CHAPTER ELEVEN

The Lord spoke to Moses, saying, "Send men to spy out the land of Canaan, which I am giving to the people of Israel. From each tribe of their fathers you shall send a man." Numbers 13:1–2

The Israelites left Mount Sinai and continued their journey toward the Promised Land. There were many other problems along the way. Again, the people grew impatient at how long their exodus was taking, and they got tired of eating manna and quail. Even the leadership of Moses was challenged by rebels, who planned to stone him to death and return to Egypt. Although the lives of Moses and Aaron were in great danger, God decided otherwise, and the rebels paid the price for opposing the ones He had selected.

When the Lord thought it was time, He commanded the Israelites to learn more about the Promised Land of Canaan to which they were traveling. Since the people were divided into twelve tribes (named after the sons of Jacob), Moses chose one man from each tribe to slip into Canaan and report on what he saw. The dozen spies did so and brought back glowing reports about the land, as well as samples of the lush fruit and other produce growing there. Yet then they added something shocking: "But the cities are so well fortified we'll never be able to conquer them."

Two of the twelve spies, however—Joshua and Caleb—contradicted them and said, "Don't believe them, and don't be frightened! Take courage! God is on our side!"

But the Israelites chose not to listen to Joshua and Caleb and instead became afraid and angry at God. As a result, God did not allow them to enter the Promised Land for forty more years.

And the exodus went onward, following God's divine plan to invade Canaan not from the south but from the east.

CHAPTER TWELVE

And there has not arisen a prophet since in Israel like Moses, whom the LORD knew face to face. Deuteronomy 34:10

Nothing about the exodus was easy, not even their entry into the Promised Land. The Israelites had to battle their way in, since people hostile to them had taken over their territory. Advancing northward along the eastern shore of the Dead Sea, they reached Mount Nebo, a lofty peak overlooking the sea. Here, there would be a dramatic change of leadership for the Hebrews.

Moses was now very old, and only a younger man could face the huge task of conquering Canaan. The man chosen was Joshua, one of the two spies who had renewed hope among the Hebrews after the ten others had tried to discourage them. It was an excellent choice because Joshua would indeed lead the Israelites to victory and to reoccupy the Promised Land.

Now God led Moses to the top of Mount Nebo so he could get a first—and last—glimpse into the Promised Land spread out before him to the west and north. His natural vision was improved miraculously so he could see it all and could die a happy man. The Lord Himself buried him in a nearby valley.

So ended the life of one of the greatest men in history. Although only one man, Moses had filled the roles of eight! Not only was he the leader of the Israelites, he was also their liberator, lawgiver, high priest, military general, strategist, judge, and representative before God. No one else could have accomplished all this, because, of course, it was God who made the entire exodus possible.

The exodus of the Israelites became the central event in the history of God's people in the Old Testament. Only the creation itself was of greater importance.

But this great story also set the pattern for how God would mount another great rescue operation for His people in the New Testament. This time, it didn't involve plagues, desert journeys, or battles, and it had a much deeper meaning.

Just as the Israelites were a complaining, disobedient, and rebellious bunch in the Sinai wilderness, so all of humanity (not just the Hebrews) is really the same way, due to their sins. Much as the Hebrews were slaves in Egypt, so men, women, and children everywhere—since Adam and Eve—have been enslaved to sin. And because of its fatal consequences, this slavery was—and is—worse than anything the Hebrews suffered.

The parallel continues. It was God who saved His chosen people from slavery through Moses, much as He would save all of His people through someone even greater than Moses—Jesus Christ. Moses would die for his people on Mount Nebo, while Christ would die for all people on Mount Calvary.

Clearly, we have a God of mercy who saves. In fact, this is exactly what the name Jesus means: "The Lord saves!"